A Little Book of House Messing

FENG SHITE

A Little Book of
House Messing

FENG
SHITE

ANNA CROSBIE

BOXTREE

First published 2001 by Boxtree
an imprint of Pan Macmillan Ltd
Pan Macmillan, 20 New Wharf Road, London N1 9RR
Basingstoke and Oxford
Associated companies throughout the world
www.panmacmillan.com

ISBN 0 7522 6149 5

1 3 5 7 9 8 6 4 2

A CIP catalogue record for this book is available from
the British Library.

Typeset by Dan Newman/Perfect Bound Ltd
Printed by The Bath Press, Bath

House Messing *vb.* 1 the process of creating a mess in one's house. *(antonym)* 1. the antithesis of house cleaning.

Mess *n.* 1 a state of dirty or unpleasant untidiness.

Instead of rearranging stuff in your house to improve your inner harmony (or whatever), try the equally ancient art of House Messing. This definitive guide is packed with simple and practical tips, and will change your life for ever! (It will certainly change the lives of those you live with . . .)

EENIE MEENIE MINIE MO

Aim to have at least six different bottles of shampoo and conditioners open and in use at any one time.

LET THEM DO IT

A key advantage of married life is the 50 per cent reduction in your obligation to change the sheets.

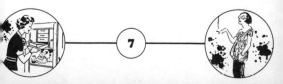

PONGY MESS

Never wash out your cans
properly before you put them in
your recycling bag. This way they
will start to smell quite nicely
within a few days.

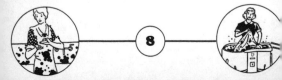

CREATING BALANCE IN YOUR ENVIRONMENT

Use the top of the wardrobe to build a structurally challenged pile of things you might one day either throw away or store in the loft.

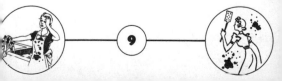

NO CLEAN CUPS?

Purchase extra supplies of mugs, teaspoons and knives. They will equip you to survive an extra day before having to wash up.

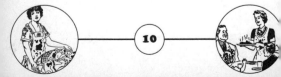

THE PHYSICS OF MAXIMUM DAMP

Remember that towels dry better hanging horizontally.

POT PLANTS

Kill them. Leave them in situ for six months before burial.

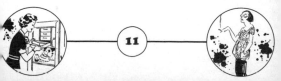

YOUR HOLIDAY UNPACKING FORMULA

$$\frac{x\,(x+2)}{3} = y$$

x = the number of days you were on holiday

y = the number of days you leave your half-unpacked suitcases and toiletry bags scattered throughout the house

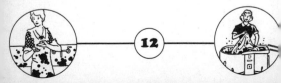

HAVE A 'THINGS PENDING' WALL

Bookshelves make an ideal holding pen for miscellaneous chores – items, for example, you intend to file some day, return to the shop for a refund, fix, or post to your cousin in Australia.

WHEN THE PAPER RUNS OUT . . .

Leave empty loo rolls on the toilet floor. They will eventually make their own way to the rubbish bin.

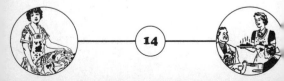

FLOWER POWER

Keep bouquets in their vases long
enough to ensure that the leaves
and petals drop onto the floor.

DISH MOUNTAIN

'This needs soaking' is a House
Messing mantra.
Use and abuse it.

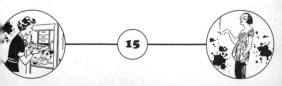

IN HONOUR AND MEMORY
OF THY MISSING LIDS

Religion is an important
cornerstone of Feng Shite. Make
your bathroom windowsill a
shrine to lidless tubes of
toothpaste.

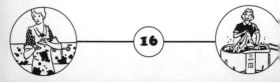

COFFEE TABLES

Buy one with a lower shelf designed to display posh, oversized photographic books (*Big Cats Close Up* and *New York Loft Architecture* type of thing). Use the lower shelf to create an 8ft² living sculpture called *I Think My Lost Car Keys Are In There Somewhere.*

FENG FRIDGE

Cover your fridge door with magnets, memos, alphabet sets, shopping lists, favourite greeting cards and cartoon strips. This will replace a clean, white empty surface with a random visual explosion – Feng Shite at its finest.

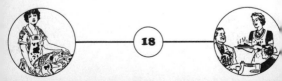

FEE FI FO FENG

Growing seeds is such fun! Nurture some herbs on your windowsill in little terracotta pots. The herbs won't grow and the soil will turn fantastically damp and mouldy. If you're lucky some spiders might move in, or a cigarette butt.

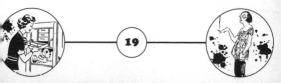

ELIMINATE GRATUITOUS CHORES

The bath sees more fresh water than any other household object or surface. It is therefore self-cleaning.

PETS

Long-haired varieties are best. (Though budgies and camels are also good.)

20

THE MODERN ELEMENT

Fire, Earth, Wind and Water are all fine and dandy, but House Messers prefer Plastic! Save supermarket carrier bags as if your life depended on it.

NEWSPAPERS

Buy weekend edition papers *every*
Saturday and Sunday. Leave the
Saturday edition scattered over the
table until you read it on
Wednesday. Leave the Sunday
edition scattered on the lounge
floor until you read it on Friday.
Leave the supplements from both
in the toilet until someone else
removes them.

PENS

Never, EVER throw one out.

PILE & DUMP

Use piles to collect and store dirty laundry. Studies show that beneath the door of the washing machine, the foot of your bed, and any spot on the bathroom floor work best.

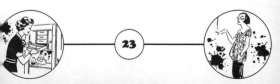

BABIES

Have as many as possible.

TOYS

Only buy huge, obtrusive toys,
made of garish, primary-coloured
pieces of plastic.

'I'M DAMNED IF I'M PICKING *THAT* UP!'

Though toys with zillions of pieces are also good; try large tubs of Lego and little wooden train sets.

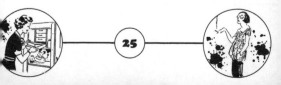

WHEN YOU DON'T KNOW WHERE ELSE TO PUT IT

Place a large bowl next to the telephone as an exclusive home for your keys. Fill the bowl instead with not-sure-if-these-are-used-or-not batteries, paperclips, discount vouchers, phone cards, some staples, one shoelace, a screwdriver, nail clippers, three stamps, a box of matches and a broken doorknob.

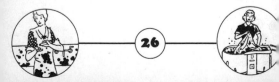

CHILDREN

Tell them that mess is cool. Tell
them they are responsible for
making their own mess.

BORROW THEM IF YOU
HAVE TO

If you haven't babies or young
children of your own, it helps to
have someone else's visit once in a
while.

CUPBOARDS

Are not for storing things. They are for hiding things.

WARNING! COULD BE TIDY IF MANAGED BETTER

Never put CDs back in their correct cases. This will create hours of fun for your anally retentive loved one.

FENG LAUNDRY No. 1

1) Leave clean laundry in a pile (somewhere) to await folding.

2) Leave pile so long that you retrieve and wear most of it before you fold it.

3) Throw the remnants of the clean pile into the airing cupboard.

IRONING

Don't provide your iron and ironing board with a permanent home. This ensures they will be constantly up and visible, somewhere.

CLUTTER

One can never own too many coasters or cushions.

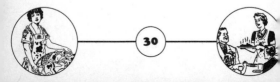

FENG SHITE FOR LIFE

Post is a free House Messing Ingredient. Send away for just one catalogue and as if by magic your name will be on every junk-mail mailing list in the country.

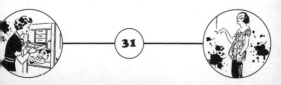

I WONDER WHAT THAT'S OFF?

If in doubt, keep it. One never knows when the World Screw Shortage Crisis will kick in.

VACUUMING

Vacuuming is pants: don't do it.

BUT IF YOU MUST . . .

Vacuum just one or two rooms, then leave the vacuum cleaner out in a *really annoying place*, on the pretence that you will finish other rooms later.

. . . AND BE DIM

Vacuuming is more fun if you never empty the dust bag.

THE HIDDEN BENEFIT OF RECYCLING

It is more *auspicious* to have large or high objects behind your house rather than in the front. On hearing this most people run off and plant a leylandii hedge. But House Messers know it's much easier and cheaper just to stack your recycling boxes (a.k.a. 93 glass jars and bottles and 17 tonnes of newspapers) at the *rear* of your house.

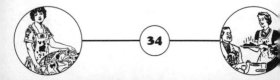

VERTICAL PILING

Every home needs a wall-mounted
notice board. If you need some
ideas for things to put on it (and
we're sure you won't), try menus,
eclectic business cards, expired
supermarket reward scheme
vouchers, inspirational recipes,
and mystery post-it note phone
numbers. Cull the contents only
when drawing pins become
dysfunctional.

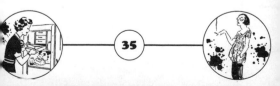

PHOTO OVERLOAD

Every time you develop a roll of
film, leave your favourite two or
three snaps propped up against the
nearest ornament on the nearest
shelf.

BELIEVE IN THE AFTERLIFE

Convince yourself that all household oddments and cast-offs should be saved for a future use that is not yet thought of, but is bound to present itself one day. Accordingly, hoard buttons, string, and bread ties with conviction.

BREED HANDBAGS

Operate several handbags consecutively. Have a different one for work, formal and casual occasions. Let them all hang out in different rooms as they wait for their next outing.

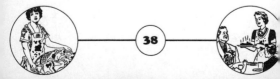

SAVOUR THE FLAVOUR

Retain used coffee granules in the bottom of your Bodum for a minimum of two days.

BUBBLE WRAP

Is an endangered species! Save all used bubble wrap regardless of how much you already have saved and how little space you have in which to store it.

ALLOW YOUR PETS TO SCAVENGE (BEFORE THE GOVERNMENT BANS IT)

Pets that scavenge are more likely to deposit the following on your carpets: remnants of dead, small, furry or fluffy critters; mud and soil samples from recent expeditions; and a selection of local leaves, grasses, cobwebs, and insect wings.

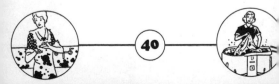

DON'T BE ASHAMED

Remember that dishwashers are for storing dirty dishes as well as cleaning them.

GET *MORE* CLUTTER

Ornaments can squeeze into the smallest of spaces. The more you have, the less appealing dusting will be.

LIVE BY LOGIC

The following are happiest living
on the kitchen bench – never put
them away:

the can opener

the Clingfilm

the paracetamol

your sunglasses

all the bits of the blender.

STORAGE SYSTEMS

Are great! You still won't put things away.

1. The tarted-up shoe boxes you've paid a fortune for will remain mostly empty.

2. Meanwhile they will add a whole new stratum of clutter to the room.

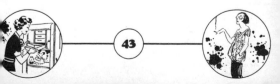

HAVE USELESS AIDS

Buy one of the many absolutely useless mops available these days. Then when you do mop the floor, it won't look any cleaner anyway.

THE LAYERED LOOK

Exploit the drying potential of
every wall-mounted radiator.

CHAIRS

Were made for hanging
coats on.

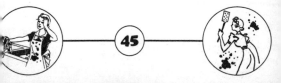

ACCEPT DEFEAT

Don't bother trying to figure out
how used teabags might make it to
the rubbish bin without dripping
all over the floor.

OUR FAVOURITE
INVENTION

Buy a duvet. Duvet owners need
never make the bed.

SPRING

Is for daffodil picking, the consumption of chocolate Easter eggs, and inaugural Sunday walks without one's hat and gloves. *Spring Cleaning* is in fact a keep-active-therapy for people in need of a life.

BEDROOM POSITIONS

Placing your bed in the corner of
the bedroom diagonally opposite
the entrance is auspicious. Sleeping
with your head towards the east
maximizes the flow of *chi* and will
ensure restful nights.
But most importantly . . .
placing a large armchair directly
adjacent to your wardrobe means
you'll never have to put your
clothes away again.

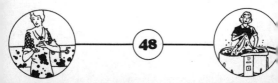

THE DOOR MAT

Never use it.

PETS HAVE FEELINGS TOO

Make sure their feeding bowls are inside.

THE FRUIT BOWL

Put your new, fresh fruit on top of
old fruit that will decay
imminently.

FENG SHOES

Just let them park and rest
wherever they want to.

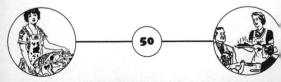

DE RIGUEUR

These things you *must* own! They have a House Messing capability all of their own and will require little effort on your part:

Sofa throws

Socks

Bath mats

Soap holders

SIZE DOES MATTER

Buy a very small bedside cabinet, with barely enough surface space for a lamp. Your clock, tissues, book, glasses, and bedroom naughties will have to colonize the carpet instead. Left to their own devices they will lay claim to territory under the bed too.

I'LL DEAL WITH THAT LATER . . .

Leave all post scattered for at least one week in the place where you first opened it.

. . . IF I CAN FIND IT

Never put today's post in the same place as yesterday's.

DIY...

Never finish what you start . . .

... MEANS 'DONE IT YET?'

Leave your hammers, tape measures, paint brushes and stepladder lying around until you do finish.

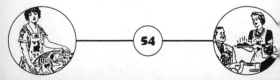

No. 1 PUBLIC ENEMIES

The most virulent House Messing efforts can be rapidly undermined by the effects of these enemy agents:

The smell of furniture polish

James Dyson

Impending visits from your mother-in-law.

Beware and avoid if you can.

FENG FOOD

Avoid sitting at the table to eat or
drink. This makes it easier
to leave mugs by the side of
the bath, cereal bowls on the
bedroom floor, and the tomato
ketchup and pepper next to
the sofa.

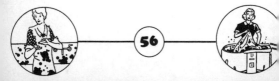

HAVE MULTIPLE WEALTH CORNERS

Reserve a flat surface area of at least 10cm² in every room for dumping loose change.

A BIG ISSUE

Cobwebs are the intricate and sophisticated labour of love of helpless and minuscule creatures. They are also their home. Leave them alone.

NON-MAINTENANCE

Delay the replacement of broken light bulbs. Their lack of function will heighten your home's general ambience of indifference.

CREATE FUTURE ARCHÆOLOGY

Preserve in your bathroom cabinet every lipstick and nail varnish you have ever owned.

BACK PORCHES

Don't have one. Your muddy boots, wet umbrellas, collapsed strollers, walking sticks and other sundries will be forced to create havoc elsewhere in the house.

MOST EASILY MESSED SURFACES AWARDS

1st Prize to cream carpets.

2nd Prize to tiles with deep-valley grouting.

3rd Prize to sea grass matting.

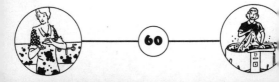

HO HO HOARD

The Christmas season provides
fertile House Messing fodder. Start
hoarding piles of gift wrap,
decorations, presents and edibles
in September.

CHRISTMAS TIDYINGS

Get a real Christmas tree with
guaranteed Hoover-proof needle
drop.

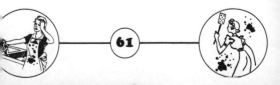

THIS ONE'S DEAD SIMPLE

Don't bother donating unwanted clothes and household bric-a-brac to charity shops. Keep everything. When you die your relatives will give it to a charity shop for you.

MAKE YET ANOTHER PILE TO BE ACTIONED

Collect used stamps for your local church charity.

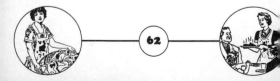

FUNCTION 1
PRETENTIOUSNESS 0

The mantelpiece aspires to be a grand architectural feature. Such aspirations are easy to quash. Use yours as a functional shelf on which to store wedding invites, old postcards, champagne corks, a bowl of stale peanuts, fourteen different candles, and the VCR manual.

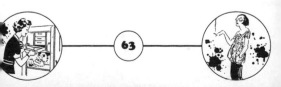

@#~* POTS!!

If treated properly, pot carousels can be a most useless storage solution and a brilliant House Messing aid. Make sure you have at least one in your kitchen. Create an impenetrable mass of pots, lids, graters, tins and trays; it will evolve into an unstoppable cascade each time you try to use it.

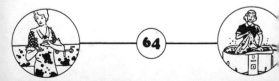

BATHING ACCESSORIES

Austerity need not apply to modern bathing conditions. Surround your bath with the leisure accessories of your dreams – loofahs, inflatable pillows, foam letters, and floating glass holders, for example. Watch them increase the surface space available to mildew and various bath scums.

SAVE MONEY WHILST CREATING HOUSE MESS

Buy in bulk! The gigantic boxes of detergent, multi-packs of kitchen towels and the 'extra 500 grams free' box of Rice Krispies will be too big to fit on your shelves. You'll have to leave them out in a really impractical and conspicuous place.

WE ♥ CRUMBS!

Place your toaster where it can be most easily knocked.

BRING YOUR INSIDE OUTSIDE

Your garden is but an additional room of your house. Treat it accordingly, and leave it to grow in whichever state and style of Mess it prefers.

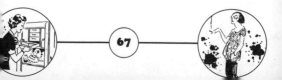

GET SUSTAINABLE!

Start a compost heap and keep a scraps bowl by the kitchen sink. There is something very risqué about decomposing House Mess.

I'M BORED OF THIS NOW

Constantly start new hobbies and quickly learn to dislike them. Their incomplete creations make a unique breed of House Mess.

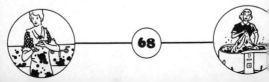

WORK FROM HOME!

1. Create an office in an inadequate corner of an unsuitable room.

2. Stack an inappropriate amount of computer paper, envelopes and fax rolls on an inadequately sized shelf.

3. The rest will take care of itself.

OFFICE FILING SYSTEM

Don't have one.

BAN CUPBOARD CULLS

Ignore expiry dates. The most
fertile breeding grounds for
superfluous objects are spice racks,
baking cupboards, and medicine
cabinets.

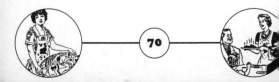

THE BLACK HOLE

You need only consider your oven's cleanliness when its use triggers off all smoke alarms and the billowing by-products of its caked interior threatens to asphyxiate you. You then have two options:

1. Get in an industrial cleaning service for a day.

2. Buy a new oven.

DUPLICATE

Don't throw out last year's editions of the phone directory and Yellow Pages when the new ones are delivered.

MAGAZINE RACKS

The more you own, the more compelled you'll be to keep ridiculous quantities of obsolete and trashy magazines.

GET FIT & FANATICAL

Buy an abdominal cruncher and an exercise bike. Regardless of how often or not you use them, you will never fold them up for storage, and you will eventually succumb to their suitability for the hanging or drying of clothes.

HAT TRICK AWARD

Have an open fire. They necessitate three of the finest House Messing attributes yet discovered by man:

Coal scuttles

Wood baskets

Ash.

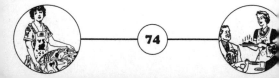

ENCOURAGEMENT

Three simple reasons to adopt
House Messing as a lifestyle
choice:

- more time to eat

- more time to drink

- more time to sleep,

FLAUNT YOUR ACHIEVEMENTS

The skirting boards and covings in the loo are easily scrutinized by visiting eyes. For the maximum promotion of your House Messing abilities, ensure they are the last surface to be cleaned of dirt, grime and cobwebs.

INEVITABLE MESS

Windows + Condensation =
MILDEW

(White or cream curtains display
mildew best)

COAT RACKS

Are for the permanent storage of
old coats you will never wear
again.

THE 'CRAM IT ALL IN' THEOREM

Fill the cupboard under the kitchen sink with three times more Tupperware containers, rubbish bags, light bulbs and shoe polish than should ever physically fit. Select items will then fall onto the floor with joyous, reckless abandon every time you open the door.

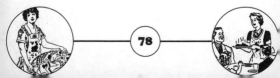

HUNT & GATHER

Scavenge shells, pebbles and other natural oddments for display in the bathroom. They will collect dust, possibly mould, and won't look anything like those in the 'Design Ideas for Your Home' article that inspired you.

GET SENTIMENTAL

Dry that special bunch of roses
and hang it upside down with a
ribbon. It will warm the cockles of
your heart with its associated
memories, whilst handily looking
to others like just more tat.

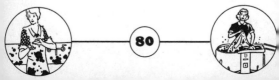

PEG BASKETS

Buy one of those Magic ones: the ones pegs jump out of.

THIS LITTLE PIGGY

Had toenails that went 'Wee Wee Wee!' all over the carpet, or the bathroom floor tiles, or the sheets.

SPORTS KIT THEOREM

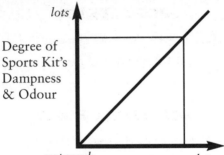

lots

Degree of
Sports Kit's
Dampness
& Odour

not much | *lots*

Time it takes to remove
kit from sports bag and
place in washing pile

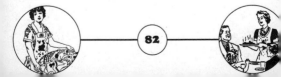

OVEN GLOVES

Are designed to hang neatly on the oven rail. Ensure your oven door is permanently stuffed with surplus teatowels, and there will never be room for your oven glove.
See how easy this is?

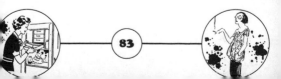

MEN CAN DO IT TOO

Men often proclaim that females are *far* superior at House Messing than they are.

Men are reminded that disposable razors do not by nature of their name require immediate disposal. Keep up to twenty used ones* in or around the toothbrush holder.

---

*The author's Husband argues profusely that razor collections are nearly always filled with *female* leg hair. Oh well, worth a try.

VEGETABLE PUEEEEW!

Did you know that if you store
your potatoes and onions in the
same vegetable rack, the onions
will emit a chemical that makes
your potatoes spoil faster?
You do now!

HARMONIZING YOUR INNER & OUTER SPACES

Keep stale bread *inside* your bread bin, and fresh bread *outside* your bread bin.

GEE UP!

The Indoor Clothes Horse was surely invented by a fanatical House Messer! Use one all year round.

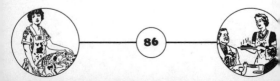

SHOW OFF

Running out of ideas for new house clutter? Hunt out any old academic, hobby or sporting related medals and trophies, and make a mini-shrine to your redundant talent.

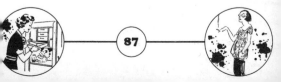

COAT HANGERS

Are another household item with a predisposed, genetic inclination to roam freely between all rooms of your house. When the shop assistant says 'Would you like the hanger with that?' always answer, 'Yes, please!'

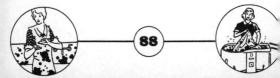

LEAVE YOUR WORK
STRESS NEAR THE DOOR

It is important to relax when you
get home from work. Take off
your tie or scarf as soon as you get
in the door and discard it over the
nearest (vacant) chair back.

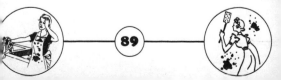

YOUR VERY OWN
CLAPHAM JUNCTION

Dedicate a lone electrical socket
around which the recharges and
cords for all the mobile phones in
your house can entwine.

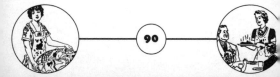

THE FUN YOU CAN HAVE WITH A CLOSE-UP PHOTO OF SOME BAKED BEANS (DISSECTED INTO 500 PIECES)!

Allocate a corner of your dining table for your jigsaw, and take a very long time to finish it.

LIVE WITH AS MANY WOMEN AS POSSIBLE

Through their ownership of make-up, perfumes, hair sprays and gels, styling combs and brushes, and hair ties and accessories, Women have a significantly greater statistical probability of destroying the bathroom.

TWO INTO ONE WON'T GO

Own twice as many utensils as there are hooks on your kitchen utensil rack.

TWO INTO ONE WON'T GO
#2

Own twice as many mugs as there are available cup hooks or mug tree spaces.

POINTS FOR EFFORT

A matching set of pretty labelled containers is an ideal present for dedicated House Messers. You know the sort: 'Tea', 'Coffee', 'Flour', 'Pasta', 'Brown Sugar'. Arrange them neatly in your kitchen and fill them with completely unrelated contents.

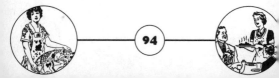

THE POWER OF PROCRASTINATION

Where possible, buy clothes that require hand washing. They will linger in your laundry for considerably longer than machine-washable items and take twice as long to dry.

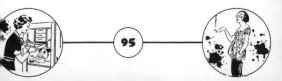

SHENG CHI

This is good chi: *a positive energy
that flows in a meandering
fashion.*

Make it by leaving your briefcase,
sports bag, or whatever else is
necessary on pertinent areas of the
floor, so it obstructs the most
direct walking routes between
rooms. *Meander* past it.

ANY OLD EXCUSE

Shar chi is bad energy. Sharp,
spiky things create *Shar chi*.
What a perfect reason to
permanently avoid your broom.

IT COULD BE YOU

Be very lax about checking your
Lottery tickets, then you will feel
obliged to keep all of them until
they become out of date.

I KNOW I HAD IT SOMEWHERE . . .

Just in case they contain a telephone number or address you might need one day, keep all your office and personal diaries from the previous five years.

98

WHAT IS DEWEY DECIMAL ANYWAY?

A subtle but effective House Messing tip . . .
Take any vertical, straight and parallel rows of books off your bookshelf, and replace them in random, leaning and perpendicular piles.

SLOPPY ADMINISTRATION HELPS

Leave all the faxes you have received or sent in the past few weeks lying beside, under or on top of your fax machine.

BONUS: This will increase your House Mess, *and* will really irritate other fax users.

100

'CAN'T DO IT PROPERLY SO THAT WILL GODDAMN DO'

Install lots of roman blinds in your house. Evidence shows that most Men are unable to operate a roman blind, and their endearing attempts to do so will leave your curtains looking suitably disarranged.

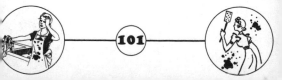

TEN GREEN BOTTLES

To compensate for the cleaning up you were forced to do for Saturday night's dinner party, leave the numerous empty wine and lager bottles it generated in a pile on the kitchen floor for at least a week.

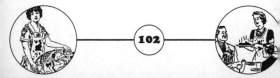

BUT IT'S WHAT MY MOTHER USED TO DO

If your dinner party leaves you with some half-full wine bottles, cork the reds and keep them on the kitchen bench. Because leftover red wine is perfect to put in a big pot of lamb stew (not that you've ever, in your entire life, made lamb stew).

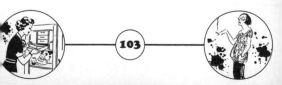

QUITE SIMPLY . . .

Life is *too* short to clean under rugs . . .

. . . FORGET IT!

. . . or behind large appliances.

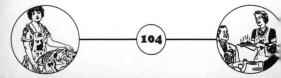

RAISE THE STAKES

Every so often, forget to put your rubbish out for the dustmen.

ARE THEY STILL ALL RIGHT TO EAT?

Wait for someone else to throw out the two stale biscuits in the bottom of the biscuit barrel.

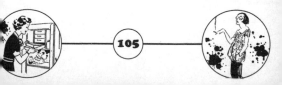

THE *REAL* INDICATOR OF YOUR HOUSE MESSING COMMITMENT

The fact that your linen cupboard isn't viewed by visitors is no excuse for keeping it tidy.

MAXIMIZE ALL CLEANABLE SURFACE AREAS

When choosing paintings and prints, remember that thick, deep frames will catch more dust and cobwebs.

MMM, I SHOULD TRY THAT

Although you're a House Messer, you're still allowed to collect an inordinate number of cleaner, polish, and detergent bottles in one of your kitchen cupboards.

WHAT'S ON?

Keep last week's *Radio Times* floating about the lounge as well as this week's.

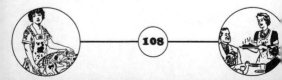

HELLO, DARLINGS

Teach the kids to dump their
school bags and lunch boxes
wherever they want.

DID YOU HAVE
A NICE DAY?

At the same time, teach the kids to
dump their coats, hats, gloves,
homework folders and library
books wherever they want.

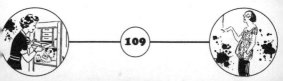

'WHY SHOULD I DO IT WHEN YOU DON'T, MUMMY?'

Finally, install in your children the value of never putting the video cassettes back in the right cases.

MUST WRITE THOSE DOWN SOMEWHERE

Because it's the only record you have of the nephew's birthday and your wedding anniversary, keep last year's calendar stuffed behind the telephone.

ORGANIZED CHAOS

Buy a large wicker tray or basket
and make it your 'Things Pending'
pile. Quietly feed and nurture it
until its contents start to spill onto
surrounding table or shelf. Tend to
its contents only in emergency
situations – before dinner parties,
or when vital pieces of household
documentation are lost.

THE 3-STEP RUBBISH PLAN

1. Buy bin liners that are fractionally too small for your bins, and without ties.

2. Rather than empty the bin, squash down the contents so that more rubbish will fit.

3. Keep squashing in rubbish until you are confident the bag will definitely split when you do lift it out.

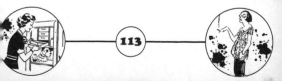

POT-POURRI

Buy lots of it. It categorically does
nothing except collect dust.

WHEN THERE'S NOTHING MUCH TO DO ON A SUNDAY

Go to a few car boot sales:
to buy more junk, not sell yours,
of course.

GET THE BIGGEST ONE

When ordering takeaway pizza always get the largest pizza; then the pizza box won't fit in the rubbish bin and will lie beside it on the kitchen floor for several days instead.

BONUS: It makes a great ashtray.

COLOUR CODING

If your hand basin is white, use blue toothpaste. The build-up of toothpaste scum will be noticeable much sooner.

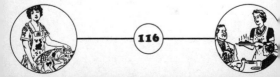

FILL IN THIS SURVEY AND YOU MIGHT WIN £10,000!

Always resolve to fill in the lengthy consumer surveys that arrive in the junk mail.
While you don't get around to it, it can lie on the dining table with everything else.

HMM, I CAN'T THINK OF A SINGLE GOOD REASON TO KEEP THESE

Your *Rough Guide* and *Lonely Planet* guidebooks are eight years out of date, and you're unlikely to ever travel to Russia, Brazil or China again, but this does *not* give you licence to throw them away.

BECAUSE FINANCIAL INSTITUTIONS CANNOT BE TRUSTED

Keep every single bank statement, chequebook stub, and credit card bill, dating back from your sixteenth birthday – in a shoe box.

BE EASILY IMPRESSED

Put into practice the handy hints
you read in the paper or see on the
telly, like keeping all your old
stockings to tie up shrubs and
tomatoes – no matter how
irrelevant they may be to your
own lifestyle.

A WINDOW CLEANING FABLE

Once upon a time there was a wise old man, who said: 'If you live in a cold, damp climate, you shall receive enough rain and condensation to rinse all dust and grime off your window panes. If you live in a warm, dry climate, your windows shall be open most of the time, so to clean them would have little consequence upon your view.' So do not bother cleaning your windows.

IT MIGHT BE WORTH
SOMETHING SOME DAY

Live in false hope that if you keep
all your phone cards, postcards
and cartoon character bubblebath
bottles, they might one day be of
value at some nondescript
Collectibles Fair.

CAR MESSING

To some people, your car will provide their first introduction to your general personal qualities. To take advantage of their confinement in a small space to promote your excellent House Messing skills, you must ensure your car is a complete tip at all times. If you've read this much of the book, it shouldn't be too difficult.

INVASION OF THE FLUORESCENT SQUARE

Buy Post-It Notes in multipacks and operate all ten pads simultaneously.

WHEN ALL ELSE FAILS

Take out a whacking great loan and build an extension. Fortunately, all House Mess associated with an extension generally comes free of charge.

HOUSE MESSING VOCABULARY:

Usage examples of key words and phrases:

avoid = 'I didn't see it!'

delay = 'I'll do it later!'

delegate = 'You do it!'

can't – 'I don't know how!'

pig-headed = 'I don't care!'

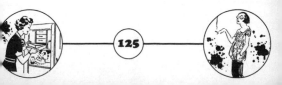

EXECUTIVE SUMMARY: HOUSE MESSING IN FIVE EASY STEPS

Take short cuts

Adore *things*: they make clutter

Have inadequate storage

Be disorganized

Hoard with religious zeal

NOTA BENE

There is a subtle but crucial difference between mess and filth. Always challenge your boundaries but never cross the threshold. Filth is disgusting!

ABOUT THE AUTHOR

Anna Crosbie was born and raised in New Zealand. She was a student for six years and a travelling nomad for some time after that. For many years therefore, her only house cleaning responsibility was to sit on her rucksack in order to get the zip closed.

She came to England in 1990 to study a Masters Degree and, although not intending to, has lived here ever since. After working in London for several years she met and married an Irishman. They decided they wanted more space to mess up so moved to Wiltshire, where they still live with their two young sons.

The author would like to stress that her Dear Mother – who will probably be horrified by this book – was in no way responsible for the House Messing habits she has developed.